WHY GOD SAID REMEMBER

Numerous surveys and questionnaires have confirmed that the most popular form of modern skepticism is to deny the creation story. Seventy-two percent of ministers interviewed expressed varying degrees of doubt that God actually spoke the world into existence according to the biblical account. This fundamental disbelief has led to the rejection of other foundational doctrines of Christendom such as the virgin birth and the atonement.

It is interesting to note that God apparently anticipated a lot of controversy over the Genesis record of fiat creation. His claims of manufacturing all the staggering mass of matter by merely commanding it to exist—well, there would certainly be doubters and disbelievers of such an account. And even those who read about it and believed it would soon forget the miraculous fact under the confusing influence of a million false gods who would arise.

So God needed to do something unusual to preserve the knowledge of His mighty act of creation. That power to speak heaven and earth into existence would distinguish Him from all the counterfeit gods and their deceptive claims. What could He do that would constantly point mankind back to the focal week of creation when He forever established His divine authority?

Creation—The Mark of God's Sovereignty

God chose to memorialize that convincing display of creative power by setting aside the seventh day of creation week as a holy day of rest and remembering. It would constitute a tremendous safeguard of God's sovereignty—a mark of His right to rule as the only true God. It would, at the same time, stand as a devastating debunking of every god who had not created the heavens and earth.

The writings of Old Testament prophets are saturated with reminders of God's peculiar powers of creation. David wrote, "For all the gods of the nations are idols: but the Lord made the heavens." Psalm 96:5. Jeremiah expressed it: "But the Lord is the true God, he is the living God. ... The gods that have not made the heavens and the earth, even they shall perish. ... He hath made the earth by his power." Jeremiah 10:10-12.

Did God Himself demonstrate an extreme urgency in keeping the truth of creation vividly before the eyes of the world? Yes. To such a degree that He wrote into the heart of His great moral law the binding obligation of every living soul to keep the Sabbath holy, and thus, to acknowledge His divine authority. Within those eternal principles forming the foundation of His government and reflecting His own perfect character, God wrote these words: "Remember the sabbath day, to keep it holy. Six days shalt thou labour, and do all thy work: But the seventh day is the sabbath of the Lord thy God: in it thou shalt not do any work. ... For in six days the Lord made heaven and earth, the sea, and all that in them is ... wherefore the Lord blessed the sabbath day, and hallowed it." Exodus 20:8-12.

What an act to highlight the omnipotent work of creation! Once a week, as the earth rotated on its axis, the Sabbath reminder would travel around the earth reaching every man, woman, and child with the message of an instant creation. Why did God say remember? Because to forget the Sabbath is to forget the Creator also.

Conversion—Creative Power at Work

Parallel to the accounts of a physical creation we find the record of God's power to recreate the human heart. Evidently, the two processes stem from the same omnipotent source. It requires just as much power to effect conversion or recreation as to call something into existence by creation. Said the apostle, "Put on the new man, which after God is *created* in righteousness and true holiness." Ephesians 4:24. Since the new birth is the most basic identifying mark of the justified believer, it is no wonder that the Bible writers constantly remind us of the creative power which distinguishes the true God from all counterfeits.

Pointing beyond the mere fact of a physical creation, God spoke these words also, "Moreover also I gave them my sabbaths, to be a sign between me and them, that they might know that I am the Lord that sanctify them." Ezekiel 20:12.

Please note that a sanctified Sabbath was to be the mark of a sanctified people. The word, "sanctify," meaning to set aside for a holy use (a day which spoke of God's creative power), served also as a reminder that God could set people apart for a holy use through regeneration or recreation.

In the light of these facts, it is easy to

understand why the devil has waged a continuing, desperate battle against the seventh-day Sabbath. For almost six millenniums he has worked through pride of tradition, misinformation and religious bigotry to destroy the sanctity of God's special sign of authority—the Sabbath.

As a mark of God's right to rule, the Sabbath challenged Satan's boast that he would take God's place. Said the adversary, "I will exalt my throne above the stars of God. ... I will be like the most High." Isaiah 14:13, 14. Satan actually wanted to be worshiped. To accomplish this, he had to nullify God's claim as the rightful ruler. God's authority rested on His claim to be the Creator, and the Sabbath was the mark of that authority. By destroying the Sabbath, Satan would prepare the way to set up a counterfeit government based on counterfeit claims of authority symbolized by a counterfeit day of worship.

The Battle Over Authority

It is fascinating to look back over the

ages and see the outworking of the great controversy between Christ and Satan. The contest has always focused upon the issue of authority.

The strategy of the evil one has been a two-pronged attack on God's claim to be the Creator. First, by the theory of evolution with its humanistic doctrine of natural selection. Second, by an age-long effort to destroy the observance of the seventh-day Sabbath, the mark of creative power.

We can only say in passing that each of these hellish attempts to discredit God's authority has produced a bitter success beyond all expectation. Millions have been turned into religious skeptics and agnostics as a result of Darwin's doctrine of organic evolution. Denying any fall of man which would necessitate a Saviour from sin, evolution struck at the plan of redemption as well as the fact of creation.

In a similar vein, Satan's attacks on the Sabbath have led millions to disobey the one commandment in the Decalogue which God had made the specific test of obedience to the entire law.

A successful plan to subvert the loyalty of millions who were devoted to the true God required a masterpiece of satanic strategy. It would take time. It would involve centuries of deceptive mind-bending. There would be no dramatic turn from serving God to serving Satan. The secret would be to win obedience through religious subterfuge. Satan understood the principle of Romans 6:16 long before Paul ever penned the words, "Know ye not, that to whom ye yield yourselves servants to obey, his servants ye are to whom ye obey?"

Obedience is the highest form of allegiance and worship. If Satan could create an issue that would cause people to disobey God, he had an even chance of winning their obedience to his cause. The decisive contest would take place over the law of God. It constituted the foundation of God's government. How could Satan destroy confidence in the law and make people obey him instead? And which commandment should he attack? Obviously, the one which pointed to God's creative power and His right to rule. As the identifying sign of the true God, the Sabbath has always been an object of satanic hate. God had chosen the Sabbath as a test of loyalty to His law in the Old Testament: "That I may prove them," said the Lord, "whether they will walk in my law, or no." Exodus 16:4.

The Test Point of the Law

Since God had made the Sabbath the test point of all the Ten Commandments, Satan determined to make it the giant issue of the ages. By destroying the Sabbath, Satan would be prepared to launch his super-plan to claim obedience to a counterfeit day of worship. Manipulating the weakness of a compromised Christianity which had slowly acceded to pagan influences, Satan set up his masterpiece—a worldwide church-state—which would ruthlessly enforce compliance with his counterfeit system of worship.

For over a thousand years, beginning with the so-called conversion of the pagan Emperor Constantine, the dark history of apostasy unfolded. Almost the first act of the newly-professed Christian emperor was to make a law against Sabbath-keeping and to institute other laws requiring rest on the first day of the week, a wild solar holiday dedicated to pagan sun worship.

We will not dwell, at present, upon the well-documented history of the papal church councils which enforced the observance of the pagan Sunday on pain of death. The facts are well-known to those who have been willing to search the records with an open mind. During the fourth and fifth centuries, the first day of the week was exalted by papal decree to displace the true Sabbath of the Bible.

Unfortunately, prejudices and false information have led thousands of Christians to close their eyes to the overwhelming historical evidences of this substitution. The roots of their prejudice are not hard to identify. Satan has worked too long on his opposition system to allow it to be rejected easily. Through the ages he has perfected a series of subtle false arguments to bolster obedience to his counterfeit day of worship. He still hates the Sabbath which identifies the true God.

Only as we expose these attacks on the seventh-day Sabbath will we be able to understand why millions continue to observe the first day of the week, a day for which there is not a single supporting Bible text. No one disagrees with the meaning of God's handwritten law, "The seventh day is the Sabbath of the Lord ... in it thou shalt not do any work." Yet millions do not obey it. No one can refute the overwhelming evidence of Sunday's pagan origin, yet millions keep it instead of the plainly commanded Sabbath of the Ten Commandments. Why? I repeat, the reason is rooted in the clever arguments of Satan which have created a climate of prejudice against the holy Sabbath of the Lord. We shall now examine some of the major fallacies of those arguments.

The Sabbath Was Made Only for the Jews

This falsehood has gained such strength

that multitudes of Christians refer to it as the "Jewish Sabbath." But nowhere do we find such an expression in the Bible. It is called "the sabbath of the Lord," but never "the sabbath of the Jews." Exodus 20:10. Luke was a Gentile writer of the New Testament and often made reference to things which were peculiarly Jewish. He spoke of the "nation of the Jews," "the people of the Jews," "the land of the Jews," and the "synagogue of the Jews." Acts 10:22; 12:11; 10:39; 14:1. But please note that Luke never referred to the "sabbath of the Jews," although he mentioned the Sabbath repeatedly.

Christ clearly taught that "the sabbath was made for man." Mark 2:27. The fact is that Adam was the only man in existence at the time God made the Sabbath. There were no Jews in the world for at least 2,000 years after creation. It could never have been made for them. Jesus used the term "man" in the generic sense, referring to mankind. The same word is used in connection with the institution of marriage which was also introduced at creation. Woman was made for man just as the Sabbath was made for man. Certainly no one believes that marriage was made only for the Jews.

The fact is that two beautiful, original institutions were set up by God Himself before sin ever came into the world—marriage and the Sabbath. Both were made for man, both received the special blessing of the Creator and both continue to be just as holy now as when they were sanctified in the Garden of Eden.

It is also interesting to note that Jesus was the One who made the Sabbath in the first week of time. There was a reason for His claim to be Lord of the Sabbath day (Mark 2:28). If He is the Lord of the Sabbath day, then the Sabbath must be the Lord's day. John had a vision on "the Lord's day," according to Revelation 1:10. That day had to be the Sabbath. It is the only day so designated and claimed by God in the Bible. In writing the Ten Commandments, God called it "the sabbath of the Lord." Exodus 20:10. In Isaiah He is quoted as saying, "The sabbath, my holy day." (Isaiah 58:13).

But we must not overlook the fact that

this God who created the world and made the Sabbath was Jesus Christ Himself. John wrote: "In the beginning was the Word, and the Word was with God, and the Word was God. The same was in the beginning with God. All things were made by him; and without him was not any thing made that was made. ... And the Word was made flesh, and dwelt among us, (and we beheld his glory, the glory as of the only begotten of the Father), full of grace and truth." John 1:1-3, 14.

Paul clearly identified Jesus as the Creator, "... his dear Son: In whom we have redemption through his blood. ... For by him were all things created." Colossians 1:13-16.

For Christians to separate Jesus from the Sabbath is a tragic mistake. For He is the Author, the Maker, the Sanctifier, and the Architect of the Sabbath. To discount the blessing which He placed on that day is to deny His authority.

This argument has led many to believe that the Sabbath existed only for a limited period of time following creation. But is this a fact? Actually, the Sabbath could never be just a type or shadow of anything, for the simple reason that it was made before sin entered the human family. Certain shadows and typical observances were instituted *as a result of sin* and pointed forward to the deliverance from sin. Such were the sacrifices employed to symbolize the death of Jesus, the Lamb of God. There would have been no animal sacrifices had there been no sin. These offerings were abolished when Christ died on the cross, because the types had met their fulfillment (Matthew 27:51). But no shadow existed before sin entered this world; therefore, the Sabbath could not be included in the ceremonial law of types and shadows.

Paul referred to the temporary system of ordinances in Colossians 2:14-16 as being "against us" and "contrary to us." He tied it to the meat offerings, drink offerings, and yearly festivals of the law that was "blotted out." It is true he referred to sabbaths also in the text, but take careful note that he called them "sabbath days which are a shadow of things to come." Were some sabbath days blotted out at the cross? Yes, there were at least four *yearly* sabbaths which came on certain set days of the month, and they were nailed to the cross. They were shadows and required specified meat and drink offerings. All of these annual sabbaths are described in Leviticus 23:24-36, and then summarized in verses 37 and 38: "These are the feasts of the Lord, which ye shall proclaim to be holy convocations, to offer an offering made by fire unto the Lord, a burnt offering, and a meat offering, a sacrifice, and drink offerings, every thing upon his day: *beside the sabbaths of the Lord.*"

The Scripture plainly differentiates between the annual, shadowy sabbaths and the weekly "sabbaths of the Lord." The ceremonial sabbaths were blotted out at the cross; they had been added as a consequence of sin. But the Sabbath of the Ten-Commandment law had been hallowed before sin was introduced and was later incorporated into the great moral law written by the finger of God. It was eternal in its very nature.

Just Keep Any Day in the Seven

By this argument Satan prepared the world to accept a substitute in place of the Sabbath God had commanded. Upon the tables of stone God wrote the great, unchanging law of the ages. Every word was serious and meaningful. Not one line was ambiguous or mysterious. Sinners and Christians, educated and uneducated, have no problem understanding the simple, clear words of the Ten Commandments. God meant what He said and He said what He meant. No one has tried to void that law as too complicated to comprehend.

Most of the ten begin with the same words: "Thou shalt not," but right in the heart of the law we find the fourth commandment which is introduced with the word, "Remember." Why is this one different? Because God was commanding them to call something to memory which already existed but had been forgotten. Genesis describes the origin of the Sabbath in these words, "Thus the heavens and the earth were finished, and all the host of them. And on the seventh day God ended his work which he had made. ... And God blessed the seventh day, and sanctified it: because that in it he had rested from all his work which God created and made." Genesis 2:1-3.

Which day did God bless and sanctify? The seventh day. How was it to be kept holy? By resting. Could any of the other six be kept holy? No. Why? Because God commanded not to rest those days but to work. Does God's blessing make a difference? Of course. This is why parents pray for God to bless their children. They believe it makes a difference. The seventh day is different from all the other six days, because it has God's blessing.

Some more questions: Why did God bless the day? Because He had created the world in six days. It was the birthday of the world, a memorial of a mighty act. Can the Sabbath memorial be changed? Never. Because it points backward to an accomplished fact. July 4 is Independence Day. Can it be changed? No. Because the Declaration of Independence was signed on July 4, 1776. Your birthday cannot be changed, either. It is a memorial of your birth, which happened on a set day. History would have to run through again to change your birthday, to change Independence Day, or to change the Sabbath day. We can *call* another day Independence Day, and we can *call* another day the Sabbath, but that does not make it so.

Did God ever give man the privilege of choosing his own day of rest? He did not. In fact, God confirmed in the Bible that the Sabbath was settled and sealed by His own divine selection and should not be tampered with. Read Exodus 16 concerning the giving of manna. For 40 years God worked three miracles every week to show Israel which day was holy. (1) No manna fell on the seventh day. (2) They could not keep it overnight without spoilage, but (3) when they kept it over the Sabbath, it remained sweet and fresh.

But some Israelites had the same idea as many modern Christians. They felt that any day in seven would be all right to keep holy: "And it came to pass, that there went out some of the people on the seventh day for to gather, and they found none. And the Lord said unto Moses, How long refuse ye to keep my commandments and my laws?" Exodus 16:27, 28.

Get the picture? These people thought another day could be kept just as well as the seventh day. Perhaps they were planning to observe the first day of the week, or some other day which was more convenient. What happened? God met them and accused them of breaking His law by going forth to work on the seventh day. Would God say the same thing to those who break the Sabbath today? Yes. He is the same yesterday, today and forever—He changes not. God made it very clear that, regardless of their feelings, those who go forth to work on the Sabbath are guilty of breaking His law. James explains that it is a sin to break even one of the Ten Commandments: "For whosoever shall keep the whole law, and yet offend in one point, he is guilty of all. For he that said, Do not commit adultery, said also, Do not kill. Now if thou commit no adultery, yet if thou kill, thou art become a transgressor of the law." James 2:10, 11.

We Can't Locate the True Seventh Day

This is a fallacy that has comforted many in their disobedience of the fourth commandment. It just is not true. Here are four positive proofs which identify the true Sabbath today:

1. According to the Scriptures, Christ died on Friday and rose on Sunday, the first day of the week. Practically all churches acknowledge this fact by observing Easter Sunday and Good Friday. Here is the Bible evidence: "This man went unto Pilate, and begged the body of Jesus. And he took it down, and wrapped it in linen, and laid it in a sepulchre that was hewn in stone, wherein never man before was laid. And that day was the preparation, and the sabbath drew on." Luke 23:52-54.

Here is proof that Jesus died the day before the Sabbath. It was called "the preparation day" because it was the time to get ready for the Sabbath. Let us read the next verses: "And the women also, which came with him from Galilee, followed after, and beheld the sepulchre, and how his body was laid. And they returned, and prepared spices and ointments; and rested the sabbath day according to the commandment." Verses 55, 56.

Please notice that the women rested over the Sabbath "according to the commandment." The commandment says, "The seventh day is the Sabbath," so we know they were observing Saturday. But the very next verse says, "Now upon the first day of the week, very early in the morning, they came unto the sepulchre, bringing the spices which they had prepared. ... And they found the stone rolled away from the sepulchre." Luke 24:1, 2.

How clearly these three consecutive days are described for us. He died Friday, the preparation day, commonly called Good Friday. He rested in the tomb on the seventh day, Sabbath, "according to the commandment." That was Saturday. Then on Sunday, the first day of the week, Easter Sunday to many, Jesus arose from the grave.

Anyone who can locate Good Friday or Easter Sunday will have absolutely no difficulty finding the true Sabbath.

2. The calendar has not been changed so as to confuse the days of the week. We can be positive that our seventh day is the same day Jesus observed when He was here. Pope Gregory XIII did make a calendar change in 1582, but it did not interfere with the weekly cycle. Our present Gregorian calendar was named after him when he made that small change in 1582.

What did Pope Gregory do to the calendar? Before 1582 the Julian calendar had been in effect, instituted by Julius Ceasar about 46 B.C. and named after him. But the Julian calendar had calculated the length of the year as 365 1/4 days, and the year is actually eleven minutes less than 365 1/4 days. Those eleven minutes accumulated, and by 1582 the numbering of the calendar was ten days out of harmony with the solar system. Gregory simply dropped those ten days out of the numbering of the calendar. It was Thursday, October 4, 1582, and the next day, Friday, should have been October 5. But Gregory made it October 15 instead, dropping exactly ten days to bring the calendar back into harmony with the heavenly bodies.

Were the days of the week confused? No. Friday still followed Thursday, and Saturday still followed Friday. The same seventh day remained, and the weekly cycle was not disturbed in the least. When we keep the seventh day on Saturday, we are observing the same day Jesus kept, and He did it every week according to Luke 4:16.

3. The third evidence for the true Sabbath is the most conclusive of all. The Jewish people have been observing the seventh day from the time of Abraham, and they still keep it today. Here is a whole nation—millions of individuals—who have been counting off time meticulously, week after week, calendar or no calendar, for thousands of years. Could they have lost track?

Impossible. The only way they could have lost a day would have been for the entire nation to have slept over an extra 24 hours and for no one ever to tell them about it afterwards.

There has been no change or loss of the Sabbath since God made it in Genesis. The origin of the week is found in the creation story. There is no scientific or astronomical reason for measuring time in cycles of seven days. It is an arbitrary arrangement of God and has been miraculously preserved for one reason—because the holy Sabbath day points to the creative power of the only true God. It is a sign of His sovereignty over the world and over human life; a sign of creation and redemption.

Is this not the reason God will preserve Sabbathkeeping throughout eternity? We read in Isaiah 66:22, 23: "For as the new heavens and the new earth, which I will make, shall remain before me, saith the Lord, so shall your seed and your name remain. And it shall come to pass, that from one new moon to another, and from one sabbath to another, shall all flesh come to worship before me, saith the Lord."

The Sabbath is so precious to God that He will have His people observe it throughout all time to come in the beautiful new earth. If it is so precious to Him, should it not be precious to us? If we are going to keep it then, should we not keep it now?

In an age of false gods, of atheistic evolution, and traditions of men, the world needs the Sabbath more than ever as a test of our loyalty to the great Creator-God and a sign of our sanctification through His power.

4. Proof number four lies in the fact that over one hundred languages of the earth use the word "Sabbath" for Saturday. For example, the Spanish word for Saturday is "Sábado," meaning Sabbath. What does this prove? It proves that when those hundred languages originated in the long, long ago, Saturday was recognized as the Sabbath day and was incorporated into the very name of the day.

The Sabbath Was Only a Memorial of Deliverance Out of Egypt

This strange idea is drawn from a single text in the Old Testament and is distorted to contradict many clear statements about the true origin of the Sabbath. The text is found in Deuteronomy 5:14, 15: "But the seventh day is the sabbath of the Lord thy God: in it thou shalt not do any work, thou, nor thy son, nor thy daughter, nor thy manservant, nor thy maidservant, nor thine ox, nor thine ass, nor any of thy cattle, nor thy stranger that is within thy gates; that thy manservant and thy maidservant may rest as well as thou. And remember that thou wast a servant in the land of Egypt, and that the Lord thy God brought thee out thence through a mighty hand and by a stretched out arm: therefore the Lord thy God commanded thee to keep the sabbath day."

Some people draw from this text that God gave the Sabbath as a memorial of the Exodus from Egypt. But the Genesis story of the making of the Sabbath (Genesis 2:1-3) and the wording of the fourth commandment by God Himself (Exodus 20:11) reveals the Sabbath as a memorial of creation.

The key to understanding these two verses rests in the word "servant." God said, "Remember that thou wast a servant in the land of Egypt." And in the sentence before this one He reminds them "that thy manservant and thy maidservant may rest as well as thou." In other words, their experience in Egypt as servants would remind them to deal justly with their servants by giving them Sabbath rest.

In similar vein God had commanded, "And if a stranger sojourn with thee in your land, ye shall not vex him ... for ye were strangers in the land of Egypt." Leviticus 19:33, 34.

It was not unusual for God to hark back to the Egyptian deliverance as an incentive to obey other commandments. In Deuteronomy 24:17, 18, God said, "Thou shalt not pervert the judgment of the stranger, nor of the fatherless; nor take a widow's raiment to pledge. ... Thou wast a bondman in Egypt, and the Lord thy God redeemed thee thence: therefore I command thee to do this thing."

Neither the command to be just nor to keep the Sabbath was given to memorialize the Exodus, but God told them that His goodness in bringing them out of captivity constituted a strong additional reason for their dealing kindly with their servants on the Sabbath and treating justly the strangers and widows.

In the same way, God spoke to them in Leviticus 11:45, "For I am the Lord that bringeth you up out of the land of Egypt. ... ye shall therefore be holy." Surely no one would insist that holiness did not exist before the Exodus, or that it would be ever afterwards limited only to the Jews, to memorialize their deliverance.

Keep Sunday in Honor of the Resurrection

It is true that Jesus rose on the first day of the week, but nowhere is there the slightest intimation in the Bible for anyone to keep that day holy. The basis for Sabbathkeeping is the direct handwritten command of God.

Many wonderful events occurred on certain days of the week, but we have no command to keep them holy. Jesus died for our sins on Friday. That is probably the most significant event in all of recorded history. It marks the moment my death sentence was commuted and my salvation assured. But not one Bible text hints that we should observe this day of such great significance.

It was a dramatic moment when Jesus rose from the grave on that Sunday morning, but there is not a scintilla of biblical evidence that we should observe it in honor of the resurrection. Not one instance of Sunday observance has been found in the recorded Scriptures.

There is, of course, a memorial of the resurrection commanded in the Bible, but it is not Sundaykeeping. Paul wrote: "Therefore we are buried with him by baptism into death: that like as Christ was raised up from the dead by the glory of the Father, even so we also should walk in newness of life." Romans 6:4.

Baptism is the memorial of Christ's death, burial and resurrection. Those who believe that Sunday observance honors His resurrection cite the upper room meeting of the disciples on the same day He arose from the grave. To them that gathering was to celebrate His resurrection. But when we read the Bible record of the event, we discover that the circumstances were quite different. Luke tells us that, even though the disciples were confronted with the eyewitness story of Mary Magdalene, they "believed not." "After that he appeared in another form unto two of them, as they walked, and went into the country. And they went and told it unto the residue: neither believed they them. Afterward he appeared unto the eleven as they sat at meat, and upbraided them with their unbelief and hardness of heart, because they believed not them which had seen him after he was risen." Mark 16:12-14.

Obviously, none of those upper room disciples believed that He was raised, so they could not have been joyously celebrating the resurrection. John explains their reason for being together in these words: "The doors were shut where the disciples were assembled *for fear of the Jews*." John 20:19.

Thus, we have examined the major arguments used against the observance of God's holy Sabbath day. Not one of the objections provides a trace of evidence that God ever changed His mind about the Sabbath. When He wrote the word "remember" into the fourth commandment, it was in reference to the same seventh day that appears on our wall calendar. Neither men nor demons can diminish the validity of that eternal moral law.

May God grant each one of us the courage to honor the Sabbath commandment as heaven's special test of our love and loyalty. As we have discovered, when Jesus returns, we will keep that same Sabbath with Him, ages without end. Even so, come, Lord Jesus.